Things to
with Kids

Tips for visiting Pigeon Forge, Gatlinburg, and the Smoky Mountains

Nick Weisenberger

Copyright Information

Table of Contents

About this Guide

The Smoky Mountain region is an amazing place to visit: majestic views, wonderful wildlife, thrilling rides, and relaxing walks are all to be found and enjoyed. Activities include relaxing, hiking, shopping, people watching, crafting, backpacking and more. You'll find something to suite every family member's needs or interests. This handbook will give you the tips and information you need to explore this popular and picturesque region with confidence.

If you don't have time to sort through a 1,000+ page manual then this book is for you. I've broken this guide up geographically into three main regions (from North to South): Pigeon Forge/Sevierville, Gatlinburg, and the Great Smoky Mountains National Park (GSMNP). The attractions listed are only ones I have had experience with myself and would personally recommend to my close friends and family. There may be other really great attractions that I haven't had the opportunity to experience yet. This guide is not meant to be all encompassing; I do not cover every single attraction in the area. The purpose is to highlight a few individual family-oriented attractions that, in my opinion, are well worth a visit.

Besides highlighting fun attractions, I also share tips to make your visit better, either by maximizing your time or dollars – usually the two biggest limiting factors from turning a good vacation into an epic vacation. Each attraction listed will have one of the symbols shown below to indicate which ones are currently free versus which ones cost money:

FREE = $0
$ = $1-$20
$$ = $21-$49
$$$ = $50+

The dollar signs represent the approximate price per person. To clarify, FREE is with regards to a general entrance or participation fee; there may be other upcharge activities at his location. Any prices listed are subject to change at any time and I only list them here as a quick reference. To get more detailed information on the exact cost of an attraction you should visit the attraction's official website (listed in the appendix).

Tip: You should almost never have to pay full price for anything in Pigeon Forge and Gatlinburg. There are discounts to be had everywhere as long as you're prepared. Most hotels and attractions have stands of coupon books where you can save a couple of dollars off a good number of places. Also be sure to ask about AAA, military, veterans, seniors, or other discounts. In advance of your travel, you should subscribe to each attraction's website, Facebook page, social media, or email lists for special offers, promotions, giveaways, or contests. It's often cheaper to buy tickets online in advance than at the attraction's ticket booth the day of.

Where are the Great Smoky Mountains?

The majority of the Great Smoky Mountains are located in Eastern Tennessee and extend south into North Carolina. This subrange of the Appalachian Mountains makes for a picturesque background for towns like Sevierville, Pigeon Forge, Gatlinburg, and Cherokee. Some visitors may think the Smoky Mountain region is in the middle of nowhere but it really is in the middle of everywhere. A large portion of the Eastern half of the United States can drive to the Smokies in less than ten hours which is why more than twelve million people visit Sevier County, Tennessee every year.

Approximate Distance from Major Cities to Gatlinburg

City, State	Miles	Hours
Chattanooga, Tennessee	71	1.2
Charlotte, North Carolina	195	3.3
Atlanta, Georgia	197	3.3
Nashville, Tennessee	223	3.7
Columbia, South Carolina	228	3.8
Louisville, Kentucky	287	4.8
Raleigh, North Carolina	325	5.4
Columbus, Ohio	398	6.6
Indianapolis, Indiana	402	6.7
Memphis, Tennessee	436	7.3
Richmond, Virginia	438	7.3
Washington DC	489	8.2
Pittsburgh, Pennsylvania	496	8.3
Jacksonville, Florida	514	8.6
St. Louis, Missouri	530	8.8
Detroit, Michigan	555	9.3
Chicago, Illinois	580	9.7

Tip: If you're coming from the north, or looking for other places to see, I highly recommend Cumberland Falls State Park in Corbin, Kentucky, not far from the border with Tennessee and only about a two-hour drive from Pigeon Forge. Just a short fifteen- or twenty-minute detour from the highway, the impressive waterfall is famous for its mist generating rainbows and "moon bows."

Great Smoky Mountain Regional Map

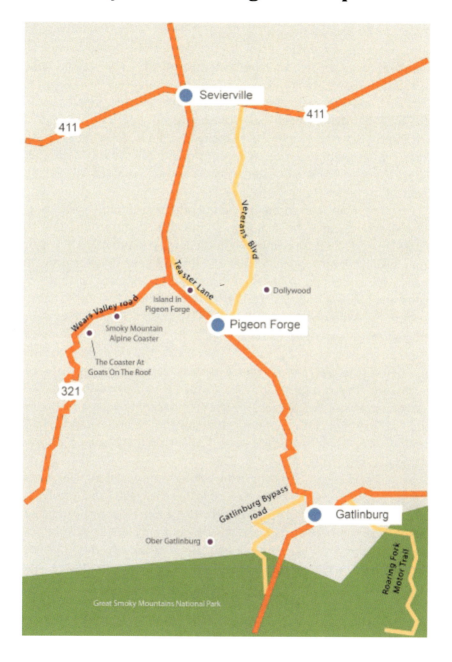

Pigeon Forge & Sevierville

Pigeon Forge is a major tourist destination in the United States and sees over eleven million visitors annually. This scenic town is surrounded by the Smoky Mountains and straddles the Little Pigeon River. Frequent travelers will see shades of other tourist destinations like Niagara Falls, Myrtle Beach, and Branson, Missouri. Besides being located just five miles north of the Great Smoky Mountains National Park, Pigeon Forge features numerous attractions including Dollywood, The Island, the Smoky Mountain Alpine Coaster, as well as several outlet malls and dinner theaters.

The main road through Pigeon Forge is U.S. Route 441, known as "The Parkway", and the majority of the tourist attractions are strung alongside of it. If you're coming from the North (as most do), the distance from Sevierville (pronounced Severe-Ville) to Pigeon Forge is only fifteen miles but it could take you well over an hour to drive due to all the traffic lights and gawking tourists. To bypass a majority of the traffic lights and tourists use Veterans Blvd. It runs parallel to US 441 and takes you past Dollywood. In Sevierville, turn from 441 onto E Main St/Dolly Parton Pkwy then turn right onto Veteran's Blvd. Veteran's Blvd runs into The Parkway just before the start of the scenic stretch of curvy road on the way to Gatlinburg. This is a great shortcut to take if you're traveling directly to Gatlinburg as The Parkway is also the main artery flowing into Gatlinburg and the Great Smoky Mountains National Park. It's also a good idea if you don't want to listen to your kids ask, "Can we do that?" about every single attraction they see off of 441.

If you're not a fan of driving during your vacation or just want to save on expensive gas money then consider using the Fun Time Trolley to get around Pigeon Forge. Trolleys run approximately every twenty minutes and stop at all the popular destinations, like Dollywood, where you'll be spared the parking toll and the long walk to the entrance – a double win! The main trolley center is at Patriot Park next to the Old Mill. The biggest downside is potentially long waits at the trolley stops and the trolleys have to deal with the same traffic as everybody else. You can ride all day for only $3.00 (exact change is required).
http://www.pigeonforgetrolley.org/

Tip: Pigeon Forge is home to various car shows throughout the year (from March through September) and with them they bring a lot of, well, cars. If you want to avoid the gridlock that comes with them then make sure you know the dates of the Pigeon Forge car shows. You can find the schedule here: http://pigeonforgerodruns.com/

Dollywood Theme Park ($$$)

Nestled in the foothills of the Smoky Mountains lies Dollywood, Pigeon Forge's most visited attraction. Unlike many overpriced tourist-traps in the area, Dollywood exceeds expectations and blows its visitors away with their outstanding customer service and family atmosphere. At Dollywood, you'll find a variety of attractions that will suit everyone from the thrill seekers to those who just want to enjoy a good show. They really do have something for everyone.

The main draw for thrill seekers is the white knuckle, heart pounding thrill rides. While Dollywood may not have as many roller coaster as other famous amusement parks in terms of quantity, they make up for it in quality. Dollywood's nine coasters are all very fun; there's no bad coasters here.

Blazing Fury is a nostalgic indoor dark ride themed to an 1880s town on fire with two small drops (comparable to Disney's famous Pirates of the Caribbean attraction in terms of show scenes and drop size).

FireChaser Express is a dual forwards-and-backwards launch family coaster that's pure laugh-out-loud fun. It's the perfect introduction to g-forces for thrill-seekers-in-training. After the Dollywood Express train, FireChaser is probably the second most popular ride in the park and thus has some of the longest wait times.

On Mystery Mine you'll find an 1,811-foot steel track plunging through an abandoned coal mine filled with cool little effects and flips riders upside down two times. Mystery Mine is not scheduled to open with the rest of the park in March to start the 2021 season due to new track work aimed at making the ride smoother and improving the experience. Check Dollywood's website for updates.

Thunderhead is one of the best wooden coasters in the world and takes advantage of the area's rough and tumble terrain to create a daring ride featuring a 100-foot drop and a top speed of 55 mph. Watch out for that unique station fly through!

Tennessee Tornado starts with a bang by dropping down a long tunnel carved in the mountainside before barreling through a giant loop and other inversions - short but sweet!

America's first wing coaster, Wild Eagle, seats riders on either side of the track so there is nothing but air above and below the rider as they're hurtled upside down four times. Don't miss the impressive eagle sculpture outside of the station area – it's a great photo op.

Lightning Rod is another groundbreaking Rocky Mountain Construction (RMC) wooden roller coaster — themed after a tricked out 1950s-era hot rod. Lightning Rod will launch its 24-seat trains from zero to 45 mph at an incline more than 20 stories up its lift hill to one of the ride's first airtime moments. At the crest of the hill, riders face twin summit airtime hills before tackling the daring first drop. Lightning Rod races down the 165-foot drop and propels guests along its 3,800-foot track to a top speed of 73 mph, the fastest speed for a wood coaster in the world. The $22 million coaster also marks the single largest attraction investment in The Dollywood Company's history.

Lightning Rod has been plagued with operation and downtime issues since its opening in 2016. Determined the fix the problems for good, Dollywood shutdown the coaster in Fall 2020 to replace some of the wooden topper track with steel I-beams. The park promises the ride will return to glory beginning in March 2021 with at least 90% uptime and a smoother ride experience, now truly being a half-wood, half-steel hybrid coaster.

Whistlepunk Chaser is the smallest roller coaster at Dollywood. The height requirement to ride is only 36 inches. It's nestled into a nook of Thunderhead, so if you have two children of different ages/heights, one parent could take the older on Thunderhead while the others ride

Whistlepunk.

DragonFlier is the newest roller coaster at Dollywood, opening with the Wildwood Grove expansion area in 2019. Don't let its modest size fool you. The coaster packs some surprising forces, but it's still gentle enough for most coaster riders new and old. This suspended coaster is short but fun and silky smooth.

Tip: Get to the park early and ride all the coasters before the crowds show up later in the day. Upon entering the park, go to the left toward Timber Canyon and make a clockwise journey through the park.

If you're going to Dollywood simply to ride coasters and big thrill rides you may be slightly disappointed. While they've added major new attractions the past several years, their coaster count at one point was less than half that of Cedar Point, Six Flags Magic Mountain, and other popular amusement parks, and Dollywood's ticket prices are more expensive. To get the full value you have to go for the full experience: the food, the shows, the crafts, the atmosphere, etc. There is much more to Dollywood then riding rides. Plus, it's better themed than your local amusement park.

For instance, you could spend a majority of your day watching many of the shows Dollywood has to offer. They've been voted the best theme park shows for five years in a row in Amusement Today's Golden Ticket Awards. There are at least four or five to choose from on a daily basis. Dollywood's A Christmas Carol, presented during the park's Smoky Mountain Christmas holiday event, even features a 3D hologram of Dolly Parton herself! (Note: Shows may be cancelled or moved outside during the COVID-19 global pandemic. Check the park's website for current status).

Craftsman Valley is full of mountain craft workers and demonstrations. Your family can watch glassblowers, see lye soap being made, observe candles being dipped, chat with blacksmiths, and learn from woodcarvers. They also have a Bald Eagle sanctuary inside the park where you can see these majestic birds up close in a giant aviary.

No visit to Dollywood is complete without a ride on the Dollywood Express. It's the number one theme park steam train in America in my book (yes, better than Disney's, Knott's Berry Farm, Silver Dollar City, and all the others). It's the biggest, loudest, and dirtiest of the bunch. When you see the black smoke start belching out of the smokestack, you'll know you're on an authentic, old fashioned steam train. It burns real coal so yes; you can get real cinders in your eyes. The track right out of the station is at a five-degree uphill grade and at one point in the journey reaches a six-degree incline. One could say the Dollywood Express is the hardest working train in the theme park industry today, safely pulling cinnamon bread stuffed guests up and down the mountain every day.

In order to pull the fully-loaded passenger cars uphill, Dollywood boasts the two biggest engines of any theme park train, with impressive twelve wheel 2-8-2 configurations. When the whistle blows, it's so loud it's almost offensive, and can be heard from outside the park. The total distance traversed on the out-and-back layout makes it the second longest theme park train at 2.9 miles traveled, behind only Silverwood's. The long ride gives you additional time to soak in the majestic views of the Smoky Mountains.

The train leaves at scheduled times throughout the day so you have to plan for when you're going to ride it. Some days you can enjoy a comical magic show after departing the Dollywood Express.

Tip: During the COVID-19 pandemic, Dollywood began issuing Return Time Tickets to ride the Dollywood Express due to the reduced capacity of the attraction (only loading every third row). If visiting in 2020 or later, you may want to check if this procedure is still in place upon entering the park, otherwise you may not get to ride this signature attraction.

Tip: Take advantage of the "Arrive after 3 PM and the next day's free" ticket deal. From March through October if you buy your ticket after 3 PM you can spend the remainder of the afternoon at Dollywood and return the next operating day for free. Check the park's website for the latest ticket deals.

What else does a good theme park need? Food! In fact, some guests visit Dollywood just for the food and nothing else. Dollywood won the Golden Ticket award for "Best Food" in 2012 and tied for first in 2013. I highly recommend the sausage sandwich at the Market Square and the 12-pound pie at Lumber Jack's Pizza. You can also get one-pound slices that can feed two people. They're huge! Some of the kid's meals are served with toys like Frisbees. The cinnamon bread available in the grist mill is world famous and I'm craving some right now.

Continuing with the awards, Dollywood has been voted "Friendliest" park multiple times. You'll notice it immediately. Almost everyone you come in contact with has a smile and greets you like you are their long-time friend. The ride operators and staff are the best around; they make your experience that much better. You can really tell they enjoy what they're doing and that is something you may not always see at the typical regional park.

Speaking of family friendly, Dollywood's parent swap program is great: the entire party waits in line TOGETHER. Most of the major rides have a dedicated waiting area where one parent waits while the other rides then they immediately swap places. It's very easy and convenient. Many of the restrooms throughout the park have Baby Care Centers attached that are awesome for changing and feeding infants. It's the little things like this that most guests will never use (or realize they are even there) that makes Dollywood a world class destination.

Dolly Parton herself can occasionally be seen in the park. Check the park's calendar of events before visiting. Dolly's Homecoming Parade takes place every May right down The Parkway in Pigeon Forge (so avoid driving through town during this time).

Tip: Besides the obvious (go on a weekday during the school year) one way to get an idea of how generally busy the park might be is to look at the scheduled hours. If the park is open later, they are expecting it to be busier on that day. It's a bit counterintuitive but while the park may be open less hours on a certain day, you could end up getting to do more rides because lighter attendance means shorter lines.

Throughout the majority of the year, Dollywood is arguably the most beautiful theme park in the country. But when the leaves turn color, the temperature begins dropping, and autumn descends on the Smoky Mountains it just takes the beauty to the next level. Without any additional decorations, Dollywood is already a nice park with great charm, theming, and aesthetic. But during Harvest Festival, there are pumpkins and decorations everywhere! At nighttime, the back section of the park is transformed into Great Pumpkin LumiNights.

http://www.dollywood.com/themepark

Dollywood's Splash Country ($$$)

Adjacent to Dollywood is Dollywood's Splash Country, Tennessee's largest water park, which features thirty-five wooded acres of water slides, attractions, pools and play areas all set in a unique Smoky Mountains setting. This outstanding waterpark has a little bit of everything with pools, raft rides, slides, and plenty of places to lounge around in the sun. Or for a little privacy and shade rent a private cabaña. There are more than twenty different waterslides, ranging from mild to wild thrills. The highlight is RiverRush, a water coaster that launches the rafts uphill using magnets. Inner tubes for the lazy river are provided at no additional cost. Tickets can be bought for just Splash Country or combo tickets to Dollywood and Splash Country. They do have a shuttle that goes from Dollywood to Splash Country and DreamMore Resort so if you have someone in your party that doesn't want to spend the whole day splashing, that is available. If you want to get wet this is the place. The waterpark operates Memorial Day to Labor Day; visit the official website for operating hours.
http://www.dollywood.com/waterpark

Fun Fact: Pigeon Forge has roughly 6,200 permanent residents, but visitors can boost the daily population to more than 50,000.

The Island (FREE)

The Island in Pigeon Forge (formerly known as Belle's Island) is a relatively new retail and entertainment center located in Pigeon Forge, Tennessee. Situated on an "island" in the middle of the Little Pigeon River, The Island is like a mini-Gatlinburg that's newer, nicer, and cleaner. It even features some of the same restaurants (Dick's Last Resort, Mellow Mushroom). There is a large parking lot between The Island and the LeConte Center. A tram service will take you from the lot right to the front of the hotel lobby and next to the fountain show. Spend the day or night exploring the thirty-five retail locations where you can shop for gifts, souvenirs, adult apparel, jewelry, framed artwork, housewares, sweet treats and more. Here are a few of the highlights of The Island:

Get lost in The Island Mirror Maze ($)

The Island Mirror Maze is a 3,000 square foot maze of 172 mirrors filled with tons of twists and bends. They hand-out 3D glasses at the beginning in case you want to give yourself more of a challenge. Also featured inside the Island Ruins is a high-tech Laser Maze where kids climb over and under security beams Mission Impossible style while being timed. If you have no interest in doing the maze yourself you should still check out the two-way mirror where spectators can watch and laugh as helpless victims get lost inside the maze.

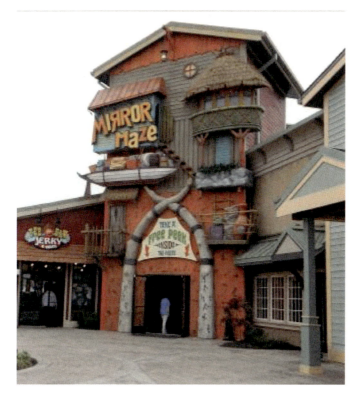

Eat at Paula Deen's Family Kitchen

Every time I go to Pigeon Forge, I just so happen to visit when a celebrity is in town, whether it's Dolly Parton, the Property Brothers, or Paula Deen – who we saw signing books in the gift shop under her new restaurant. Paula Deen's Family Kitchen is now open and features a brand new 4,000 square foot Paula Deen Retail Store and a full-service dining area. Tiered seating provides each guest a unique view of the Island's Show Fountains, along with the Great Smoky Mountains in the distance. Everything was super fresh, hot and delicious (and dessert is included!). It's one of seventeen places to eat at The Island.

Enjoy a tasty treat from Mellow Mushroom &Dude's Daiquiris ($)

The Island is home to a new quick service Mellow Mushroom where you order at the counter before taking your seat and the pizzas are brought out to you when they're done (gluten free options available). You can download a Rockbot app to your smartphone and help select the music being played. Attached to the restaurant is Dude's Daiquiris, a bar serving delicious frozen daiquiris and a large selection of craft beers. The outside patio seating area is a perfect place to relax with great views of the observation wheel, especially at night when the wheel is all lit up. Let the kids climb the ropes or ride the wheel while you relax with a good drink.

Eat Spaghetti ice cream at Poyner's Pommes Frites (CLOSED)

Kids and adults alike will love watching the creation of one of the most popular treats at Poyner's Pommes Frites - Spaghetti Ice, an ice-cream dessert made to look like a plate of spaghetti pasta. First, vanilla ice cream is scooped into a machine and comes out looking like noodles. Next, the "sauce" is poured on and is your choice of strawberry, cherry, raspberry, or chocolate. The "parmesan cheese" is made of white chocolate flakes. Ferraro Roche makes up the meatballs and two cookies are the "breadsticks." Amazing! Other specialty items include: Pommes Frites (Belgian Fries) and Dipping Sauces, a variety of authentic German Sausages and Bratwursts, and fresh baked Broetchen (German Hard Rolls).

UPDATE: Poyner's Pommes Frites closed in 2020. I've kept it in

the book for sentimental reasons and in case they re-open as there was talk of it coming back in some other form.

Watch The Island Show Fountains (FREE)

While at rest the $3 million Island Show Fountains may seem like nothing more than a fancy fountain and a relaxing place to take a break. But every thirty minutes starting at 10am the fountain springs to life in a dazzling display of water, light, and sound similar to Disney's "World of Color" or the world-famous Bellagio fountains (though on a much smaller scale). Geyser nozzles blast water over sixty feet into the air while six motion-based nozzles spray and swirl to the booming music. The 89 nozzles are perfectly synchronized to fourteen different songs. Each "show" is one or two songs long and each is performed at the same time each day. As amazing as the show is to watch during the day, where it really shines is after the sun sets. With the bright LEDs on the observation wheel in the background, it's really a sight to behold.

Ride the Great Smoky Mountain Wheel ($$)

The main attraction at The Island is the Great Smoky Mountain wheel, a 200-foot-tall $10 million dollar observation wheel. There are 42 fully-enclosed cabins capable of holding up to eight passengers at one time. The cabins are climate controlled meaning the wheel can operate all year long. Ride time varies but the duration is a minimum of ten minutes. VIP cabins are available as well, seating only four passengers at a time, they include plush leather seats and a special glass floor. And no, you cannot see Dollywood or Gatlinburg from the top of the wheel.

Tip: Get Great Smoky Mountain Wheel and Ripley's Aquarium of the Smokies Combo Tickets and save up to $6.00 per person.

Flying Theater (Coming in 2021)

Announced in February 2019, a Flying Theater attraction is due to open at The Island in 2021. The 39-seat theater will be designed and built by Dynamic Attractions; a company known for their immersive theme park attractions. The $20 million dollar theater will show a custom film transporting riders to some of America's most famous landmarks. Similar to the ever popular Soarin' attractions at Walt Disney World's Epcot and Disney California Adventure, riders will experience scents, mists, and the sensation of flight. Personally, I can't wait to ride this one with my kids!

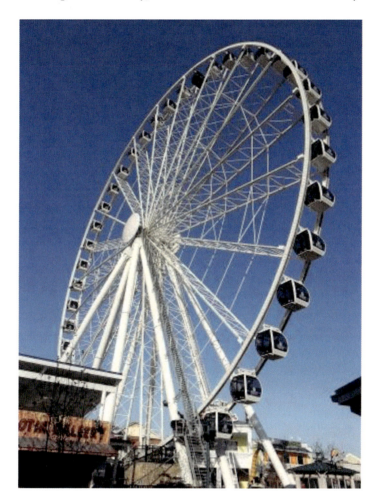

The Escape Game

The Escape Game is a fun, new entertainment concept on The Island designed for small groups of two to eight people. The goal of the game is simple: you work together as a team, testing your wits and skills, to escape from a locked room. While the goal is simple, the game is challenging. Getting through the locked door will require finding clues, solving puzzles, and working together as a team to see if you can escape from the locked room in less than 60 minutes. These types of attractions are becoming more and more popular.

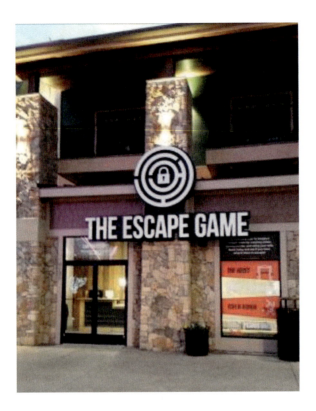

7D Adventure

Another one of The Island's sixteen attractions, and perhaps the most intriguing new attraction, is the 7D Adventure. Advertisements say you will "Experience the thrill of a roller coaster and the excitement of an interactive shooting gallery — all without leaving your seat!" The adventure includes a 3D movie with lights, sound, wind and an interactive game. The game part keeps score so that you can show off your skills.

Climb the Island's Rope Courses

Another new addition to The Island is the brightly colored Ropes Course. The towering structure is situated at the end of the complex, sandwiched between the Ferris wheel and Mirror Maze. Even if you're not into climbing, it's still fun to sit near the structure and watch the more adventurous ones make their way through the course. There are two different courses for you to choose from. One course, called Sky Tykes, is for anyone less than 48 inches tall who seeks a challenge, but may prefer to be just a little bit closer to the ground. This course has nine different elements and parents can walk on the ground beside their child for encouragement and help whenever necessary. Just like on the big course, participants are in their harness and attached to a sling line and carabiners, so they are safe and secure at all times.

For adults or children wanting a little bigger challenge, there is the three-story Sky Trail Explorer course. Anyone over 42 inches tall can tackle the course, but if you are under 48" tall, you will need a taller chaperone to go with you. With thirty different elements, two zip lines, and one simulated free fall (Quick Jump), participants have many options. There is no time limit and when you are ready to finish either walk back down the stairs or use the Quick Jump. Sounds like fun!

Other rides at The Island include the Spinning Parrots Coaster, carousel, and more kiddie style spinning rides. Young or old, The Island is a great place to visit and offers something for everyone.

http://islandinpigeonforge.com/

The Old Mill (FREE)

No Smoky Mountain vacation is complete without a quick stop at The Old Mill. This historic gristmill was built back in 1830 and is still running today. Visitors can dine on classic family favorites such as country-fried steak and pot roast before watching meal and flour being ground by the iconic mill. Attached to the restaurant is the General Store, where over a million shoppers a year hunt for tasty treats such as the homemade jams, jellies, fudge, salad dressings, and other popular products.

Outside, kids can feed the ducks and pigeons that are always hanging out along the banks of the river. Or bring your fishing pole to see if you can catch anything in the river. Pottery and ice cream can be found at adjacent stores in Old Mill Square which is also home to the main stop for the Fun Time Trolley.

If you don't snap a picture of your family in front of the Old Mill, did you ever really even go to Pigeon Forge?

http://www.old-mill.com/

Riverwalk Greenway (FREE)

Adjacent to The Island and Old Mill is the Riverwalk Greenway. This new trail has become very popular with locals as it provides a peaceful walk along the Little Pigeon River near the parkway in Pigeon Forge (though on parts of the opposite bank you will see the ugly backside of all the buildings along The Parkway). It's about a 2.5-mile-long trail that connects The Island in Pigeon Forge with Patriot Park and the Old Mill. If you're looking to get some exercise, you could start at one end of the trail, walk to the other for lunch, and then walk back. If you walk to the Old Mill, I suggest lunch at The Old Mill Pottery House Café & Grille and if you walk to The Island, then try the Timberwood Grill.

Tip: Another shortcut you can use to bypass some of the congestion is Teaster Lane that also runs parallel to US 441. It's great for accessing places like the Old Mill and The Island.

Alpine Coasters

At the rate they keep materializing, the Smoky Mountain Region should be known as the alpine coaster capital of the world. Prior to summer 2013, there were no alpine coasters to be found and now there are multiple rides – both in Pigeon Forge and in Gatlinburg – varying from 3,280 to a whopping 5,400 feet in track length.

What makes an alpine coaster different from your typical roller coaster? After the initial climb the track is all downhill (no going back uphill or inversions) and you have the ability to control the speed of your sled as it made its way down the mountain. However, the top speed is limited to around twenty-five to thirty miles per hour for safety reasons. There are two levers that must be pressed forward to maintain maximum speed throughout the course; let the handles lean back and you can take a slow, leisurely trip instead (but why would you?). The speed of the vehicle is also controlled by permanent brakes in the form of magnets mounted to the center of the track to automatically slow the sleds as they approach the station. And the alpine coasters operate year-round, even when there's snow on the ground.

If you're like me, the thought of tackling all of the alpine coasters in the Smoky Mountains is overwhelming. Where do you start? Which one is the best? In this guide I'm going to describe all the alpine coasters so you can decide which one you most want to try.

As you'll see, most of the alpine coasters are in the $15-16 price range. When you think that you can get into most theme parks for the price of four alpine rides, it seems pretty steep, but remember a lot of these places rely solely on ride ticket sales, not food or souvenirs, for profit. And couple that with the fact that you can't just ride these anywhere, it isn't too bad if you do a couple every time you visit the area.

Alpine Coaster Name	Location	Length (ft)	Top Speed (MPH)	Single Adult Ticket USD	Min. Rider Height (in)	Single/Adult Rider Height (in)	Opened	Manufacturer	Time
Gatlinburg Mountain Coaster	Gatlinburg	3,280	30	$16.00	38	56	2014	Wiegand	4-5 min
Ober Gatlinburg's Ski Mountain Coaster	Gatlinburg	3,750	25	$16.00	36	52	2015	APG	5.5 min
Rail Runner at Anakeesta	Gatlinburg	2,099	25	$35 ($13+$22)	38	48	2018	Brandauer	4-5 min
Rowdy Bear Gatlinburg	Gatlinburg	3,100	35	$16.00	38	54	2017	Wiegand	4-5 min
Rocky Top Mountain Coaster	Pigeon Forge	3,690	30	$18.00	38	56	2018	Wiegand	9 - 10 min
Smoky Mountain Alpine Coaster	Pigeon Forge	5,400	27	$17.00	38	56	2013	Wiegand	7-8 min
The Coaster at Goats on the Roof	Pigeon Forge	4,375	27	$15.00	38	56	2015	Wiegand	6-7 min

Smoky Mountain Alpine Coaster ($)

One of the top-rated attractions in the Pigeon Forge area on TripAdvisor and probably the best alpine coaster of the bunch is the Smoky Mountain Alpine Coaster, formerly the longest ride of its type in the US (now claimed by the Lake Placid Cliffside Coaster). As you drive down Wears Valley Road and the alpine coaster comes into view you may be surprised at how high up the steel rails tower above you. Each sled is equipped with a three-point restraint system, along with a lap seat belt for the passenger (when two riders are on the sled at the same time). After boarding one of the sleds the ride begins with a short chain lift, which is what sets the initial spacing between the vehicles. Next, you slowly roll along a bridge over a babbling brook before engaging the seemingly endless lift hill cable. After a series of inclines up the side of the mountain and into the cool temperatures of the forest you reach the summit and it's all downhill from there.

The scenic journey to the top takes more than five minutes while the trip down the mountain takes two or three resulting in an eight- or nine-minute ride. Highlights include a great, though brief, view of Pigeon Forge sprawled out below you. There are two helixes with surprising lateral forces as you spiral towards the bottom of the mountain. The majority of the track follows the terrain and seems to be only a foot or two above the ground. Combined with the close proximity of the trees whipping past you and you'll feel like you're going much faster than the top speed of up to 27 miles per hour.

The original, the longest, one of the fastest. The Smoky Mountain Alpine Coaster may easily be the king of the bunch. Its layout has about everything you like to see in an alpine ride—long swooping s-curve sections, double downs, and large helixes. The ride has two main sections, a low-to-the-ground first half that snakes along the top of the mountain and a second half that consists of all of the helixes (some that are quite high off of the ground). If you are only going to ride one, this is the one. It is the perfect blend of thrill, fun, ride length, and price per minute value.

A ride on the alpine coaster will cost one person $17 but you can find coupon books outside almost every restaurant or attraction in the area so you should be able to save at least a couple of dollars. It's still a bit steep even at $12 per ride after discounts but more than worth it to do at least once, and a better value than many of the other tourist traps in town.

The Smoky Mountain Alpine Coaster operates year-round, even when there's snow on the ground. See their official website for rider height and weight requirements:

http://www.smokymountainalpinecoaster.com/faq.html

Tip: Visit the coaster first thing on a weekday morning for the shortest lines. It also may be a good idea to call ahead to see how long the wait is. Due to only one or two passengers per vehicle, the ride's capacity is much lower than a roller coaster you'd find at a typical amusement park (and is one reason why you don't see this type of ride at an amusement park).

Goats on the Roof (FREE)

A mile down Wears Valley Road from the Smoky Mountain Alpine Coaster you'll find a unique establishment: Goats on the Roof. It gets its name because there are literally goats living on the roof of this quirky gift shop. Youngsters can even use one of several different contraptions designed to lift food up to the goats on the roof (for a small fee). It's a modern twist on the traditional petting zoo. Besides the main gift shop, you'll also find ice cream treats, Amish food and furniture, sample fudge, and go gem stone mining. It may be corny but kids will love it. Climb the stairs to the second floor of the gift shop and when you peer out a second story window a goat just might be staring back at you. A short stop here will be one of those odd fun vacation moments that your children will tell their friends about.

The Coaster at Goats on the Roof ($)

In 2014, Goats on the Roof added to the fun by opening their very own alpine coaster, dubbed "The Coaster." It's the second longest alpine coaster in the area at 4,375 feet. The ride begins by scaling the mountain hillside behind the store. From the parking lot you can see the giant helixes that you'll speed down towering above you. The person controlling the sled has to be at least 56 inches (4.6 ft) tall and at least 16 years old to drive someone else. The minimum height of the ride is set at 38 inches (3.1 ft) otherwise you could end up eating with the goats on the roof!

I view The Coaster at Goats on the Roof as the Smoky Mountain Alpine Coaster's little brother: at just over 1,000 feet shorter, The Coaster's layout is almost a mirrored version of its neighbor and that makes it a very good ride as well. Goats on the Roof is a little more off the beaten path and further away from the main road, so it may not be as busy as other coasters in the heart of the tourist areas. Don't forget to wave to the goats as you fly by!

http://www.goatsontheroofofthesmokies.com/goat-stories.php

Rocky Top Mountain Coaster ($)

The Rocky Top Mountain Coaster is one of the newest alpine coasters in the region and possibly the most unique. The ride has four lifts, four tunnels, and a bit of theming throughout the ride. This is more of an experience than a ride. You definitely feel like you're getting your money's worth with this one; the ride just keeps going. I love that from the road you can only see about a fifth of the layout and when you crest the first hill you can just see the spiderweb of track that is hiding in the hills. In ride time, Rocky Top is twice as long as most of the alpine coasters. Even though it is the third shortest of the two-rail alpine coasters, its four lift hills help pace this ride out to ten minutes. Rocky Top is also the closest alpine coaster to Dollywood, located about a mile away on Veterans Boulevard.

https://www.rockytopcoaster.com/

Rowdy Bear Pigeon Forge ($$)

The sister location to Rowdy Bear Mountain in Gatlinburg is relatively new, opening in August 2019. Rowdy Bear Ridge in Pigeon Forge has year-round tubing (on turf), a suspended coaster, and a new style of alpine coaster being built for 2021.

The suspended coaster, claimed to be America's first "Alpine Flyer", is a two-seat suspended coaster that swings, dips, and soars along the hillside. It's dubbed the Laser Gun Coaster because all riders get a chance to shoot targets along the layout of the ride. I was very impressed with the accuracy of the guns. They also had a chance to get a free ride on the Rowdy Bear Coaster in Gatlinburg if you scored over 50 points. The ride itself is fairly slow, but enjoyable, especially when you are trying to get those coveted 50 points. This coaster is suitable for riders 40" tall and up. Coaster operates day and night and can be combined with the Tubing Hill by purchasing a combo ticket.

https://www.rowdybearmountain.com/pigeon-forge/

Mini Golf ($$)

It's not officially a vacation in my family until at least one round of miniature golf is played. My personal favorite is Professor Hacker's Lost Treasure Golf. You begin your adventure by riding a train ride around the course (included in the cost) before putting your way through caves, around waterfalls, pirate ships, a temple, and a volcano. Ages four and under are free with a paying adult. You can add on a second round for just $5 (plus tax). Learn more here:

http://losttreasuregolf.com/miniature-golf-courses/pigeon-forge-mini-golf-course/

Other notable miniature golf courses I haven't personally tried yet but can't wait to:

Crave features candy and dessert themed indoor-and-outdoor 19-hole golf courses. To make it more interesting and unique, there are game spinners at every hole. If someone in your group spins a candy or ice cream icon, mark it down. If you collect 19 candies or 19 ice creams, exchange your card for a prize at the concessions counter.

https://www.cravegolf.com/

Ripley's Old MacDonald's Farm Mini-golf, located next to the Tanger Outlets in Sevierville, consists of three courses (easy, medium, hard) comprising 54 holes. This fun mini golf features animated barnyard characters, water features, and interactive elements at every turn.

https://www.ripleys.com/gatlinburg/mini-golf/

Dinner Shows, Shows, and Shops ($$)

Pigeon Forge may be the dinner show capital of the world. There's a show to suite every member of the family. There's music, comedy, magic, buffaloes, lumberjacks, horses, and dogs. If you're looking for work the theaters are always looking for singers, dancers, magicians, comedians, jugglers, musicians, equestrians, lumberjacks, and more.

The Comedy Barn is a good choice for people of any age with its variety of clean comedy, live music, dancing, acrobatic dogs, and so much more. Be prepared for a bit of audience participation resulting in every show being unique and hilarious in different ways. If you're looking for something that the entire family will love and talk about long after your trip is over, then be sure to check out the Comedy Barn. https://comedybarn.com/

The Hatfield & McCoy dinner show is located where the former Black Bear Jamboree once stood off of the Parkway and has quickly become one of the more popular dinner shows in the Smokies for their variety of live music, comedy, and tasty food. The spectacle is loosely based on infamous feud between the Hatfield and McCoy families and provides an entertaining look at "Appalachian life" with some incredibly talented musicians and dancers. **https://hatfieldmccoydinnerfeud.com/**

The Pirate Voyage Dinner and Show invites you to join the most famous pirate, Blackbeard, and his quartermaster, Calico Jack, as they lead the Crimson and Sapphire crews in a battle on land, on deck, in water and high above full-sized pirate ships in an indoor hideaway lagoon. Be amazed by beautiful mermaids, tropical birds, and much more all while you enjoy a fabulous four-course feast. Located just outside of The Island. https://piratesvoyage.com/pigeon-forge/

If country music is your thing, then be sure to check out Country Tonite featuring some of the best performers in the Smokies. This highly entertaining show features live music, dancing, comedy, and more in an award-winning show that seems to get better each year. Children even love Country Tonite as it features some incredibly talented young performers as well. https://www.countrytonitepf.com/

Dolly Parton's Stampede is the longest-lasting Dinner Show in Pigeon Forge featuring an entertaining "tribute" to the era of the Civil

War as it splits the audience into North and South sections in a friendly competition. The meal is delicious, but be advised there is no silverware or utensils provided (because cleaning the thousands of utensils required would be a logistics nightmare and using plastic would be quite wasteful).

Dinner at Stampede consists of tender whole rotisserie chicken, hickory smoked barbeque pork loin, buttery corn on the cob, herb basted potato, creamy vegetable soup, home-made biscuit, and a specialty dessert. Everything can be eaten and slurped with your hands, but it's good to know ahead of time. The show features highly-skilled equestrians, buffalo, ostriches, and even pigs. It's a fun experience for the whole family and is worth to do at least once. The food is great but as an adult I thought the show itself was pretty "meh" or average, about the same quality as a typical theme park show. The show is tweaked and "plussed" every year or two so it could be much improved since my initial viewing. Arrive an hour early for extra entertainment in the Carriage room while munching on popcorn or peanuts.

Tip: If you're looking for something to entertain the kids with and don't want to buy the pricey tickets, you can always visit Dolly Parton's Stampede during the day and see some of the horses up close in their outdoor stalls located along the perimeter of the show building. Parking in the adjacent lots is free all day.

One of our favorite shops is the Christmas Place. While not as large as the world famous Bronner's Christmas Wonderland in Frankenmuth, Michigan, the Christmas Place is the second largest Christmas store I've ever visited. We like to play a game where each child searches for and purchases an ornament for the other one.

Paula Deen's Lumberjack Feud Adventure Park & The Flying Ox Zip Coaster ($$)

Paula Deen's restaurant at The Island isn't the only attraction to bear her name. Paula Deen's Lumberjack Feud features over a dozen competitive lumberjack events featuring the Dawson and McGraw families' world class lumberjacks. Events include high-energy axe throwing, chopping, sawing, speed climbing, log rolling and other competitive events. Audience members can participate in an exciting, interactive experience on stage, with a special intermission event just for kids.

After you watch the show, compete in your own Lumberjack competitions at the all-new Lumberjack Feud Adventure Park. You can try your skills on the High Woodsman Challenge; a multi-level obstacle course. The Adventure Park also offers logger sports challenges like log rolling, speed climbing, and the boom run. Lastly, the park includes the 80-foot Timber Towers where you can try four controlled jump elements that are sure to make your stomach drop.

Pigeon Forge and Gatlinburg, Tennessee may be home to more attractions that make you ask "Is it a roller coaster?" than any other place in the world. As a coaster enthusiast, I love counting my "coaster credits" but sometimes it's hard to decide what counts and what doesn't as a roller coaster. The Flying Ox, a rail-to-zipline-to rail zipline coaster, may be the most controversial yet.

Is The Flying Ox a roller coaster? Well, for starters it coasts. It rides on a rail, though not the whole time. I believe the ride also uses magnetic brakes at the end like many roller coasters do. But you do hang in a harness like a zipline, not a solid ride vehicle with lap or shoulder restraints. And you don't ride the full circuit – you have to climb an eighty-foot spiral staircase before getting hooked up. Either way, it sure is fun to watch as daring riders scream as they sway right over your head. And that's the most important question in my mind: is the ride fun? The answer, whether you're riding or watching, is yes!

A ride on the Flying Ox is included in the $35 ticket for the entire adventure park. You can purchase only a ride on this zip line coaster. They take $10 off the full park price if that is the only thing you're wanting to do. $25 plus tax, which came out to $28 and change, which personally seems a bit steep for this attraction.

https://lumberjackfeud.com/

Gatlinburg

Gatlinburg is a quirky town nestled at the foot of the national park, the closest city to the Smokies and surrounded by shrouded peaks. The pure beauty of the area is one reason it's such a popular destination for weddings and honeymoons. As in Pigeon Forge, U.S. 441 is the main roadway running north to south through the center of town and is the main pathway into the national park. The Parkway in Gatlinburg is almost always clogged with foot and vehicle traffic and can be stressful to drive through. It's said Gatlinburg can grow to a population of 40,000-plus on any given night.

Walking the Downtown Parkway, which runs from one end of town to the other, is a must for every visitor. Park at one end of the parkway, stroll down one side of the street and back up the other, peering in all the shops on the way. Shopping and people watching are favorite activities but be warned: Gatlinburg attracts all types of people. Other attractions include a variety of haunted houses, wax museums, fortune tellers, mini golf courses.

Tip: Parking can be expensive at times. An alternative way to get around is the Gatlinburg Trolley which operates Monday through Sunday from 8:00am to midnight from April through October.

Gatlinburg's primary source of lodging is the cabin rental industry. Since their location is closer to the national park than Pigeon Forge, many of the cabins have extremely spectacular views of the magnificent mountains. The process of getting to one of those amazing views could be a bit daunting; accessing the cabin may require driving up extremely steep winding roads and narrow passages. Traveling up these mountains when you're not use to it may cause nausea and lightheadedness and could be a bit difficult during inclement weather.

Fun Fact: In the early 1800s, Gatlinburg was first name White Oak Flats after the abundant native white oak trees covering the mountainous landscape.

Gatlinburg Mountain Coaster ($)

The Gatlinburg Mountain Coaster is one of the latest thrill attractions to open in the Smoky Mountain region. Located in Gatlinburg, this seven-to-eight-minute coaster takes riders on up into the majestic Smoky Mountains for a thrilling journey just over a mile in length. The Gatlinburg Mountain Coaster can hit speeds of up to 30 mph. Come into Gatlinburg at night for the best experience; the parts of the layouts that are in the trees are not well-lit so you will have an almost pitch-black ride. The attraction cost several million dollars to build and opened in mid-September 2014. Located at 306 Parkway (Traffic Light #2) in Gatlinburg, one trip down the mountain will set you back around $16 for a single rider.

http://gatlinburgmountaincoaster.com/

Rowdy Bear Gatlinburg ($)

If you feel a need for speed, the Rowdy Bear alpine coaster is for you. Out of all the mountain coasters in the region, its top speed of 35 miles per hour is significantly higher than the next closest ride at 30 mph. In October of 2020, Rowdy Bear upped the fun factor by adding laser guns to the up-track of the alpine coaster. Laser guns operate day and night. Score the high score and win a tubing hill adventure at their Pigeon Forge location.

Rowdy Bear Gatlinburg is also home to the World's first Mountain Glider. This single-rail suspended coaster has you riding in a harness more like a zipline rather than a fixed seat. Riders must be a minimum of 80lbs to ride and a max weight of 275lbs in dry conditions and 230lbs in wet conditions.

https://www.rowdybearmountain.com/gatlinburg/

Aerial Tram to Ober Gatlinburg ($)

One way to see the magnificent sights without driving is to take the aerial tramway from downtown Gatlinburg to the Ober Gatlinburg resort. There are two enclosed 120-person trams that whisk passengers up Mt. Harrison to an elevation of 2,700 feet. One station is located in downtown Gatlinburg and the other is at the top of the mountain. The 2.1-mile journey lasts about ten minutes. If you're afraid of heights this is not for you. It really can be quite scary when the tram rocks back and forth after sliding over one of the towering support columns. It's well worth the cost of admission for the views and is a longer ride up than the Sky Lift (chair-lift style ride down the street) and is open rain or shine. Ober Gatlinburg is the only ski resort in Tennessee. The ride up the mountain is a better value than many of the attractions you'll find once you actually get to Ober Gatlinburg. Tickets are roundtrip and the tram typically operate 9:30am to 7:20pm.

Ober Gatlinburg also has other family-friendly activities, including, an ice-skating rink, ice bumper cars, snow tubing, and skiing in the winter. The staff are very friendly. Besides taking the tram, you can also drive up a very twisting mountain road, but I much prefer the tram.
http://www.obergatlinburg.com/

Ober Gatlinburg's Ski Mountain Coaster ($)

The Smokies fourth mountain coaster opened in August of 2015. Ober Gatlinburg's Ski Mountain Coaster is the third longest one. The mountain coaster departs near the Tubing Park and begins with a tranquil uphill ride through woods that border the Great Smoky Mountain National Park. You'll spiral down the slope of Mount Harrison for five-and-a-half minutes. If you're looking for a quick spin on an alpine coaster, this is not the one you want to try as it's one of the two most difficult to get to (along with Rail Runner) and will cost you extra – either to park or to take the aerial tram to the summit.

However, if you have young kids and are wanting to introduce them to alpine coasters, the Ski Mountain Coaster at Ober Gatlinburg may be the way to go. Not only does it have the shortest height requirement of all the alpine rides, at 36 inches (Wiegand models have a 38-inch height requirement), but kids ages three and four are free with a paying adult. This ride has a top speed of 25 mph, one of the slower coasters in the area, making it best for families (even though my 3-year-old was yelling "faster, faster!" the whole time). I remember getting off of this ride and thinking how great the pacing was too. From start to finish this ride held its own, with smooth transitions and the perfect amount of speed for the layout. **http://obergatlinburg.com/mountain-coaster/**

Ripley's Aquarium of the Smokies ($$)

Ripley's Aquarium of the Smokies is one of the prominent buildings of Gatlinburg and the kids will surely beg you to take them there. Located at Traffic Light #5 Downtown, the aquarium features numerous exhibits divided up into themed regions. Animals you'll encounter as you explore include giant spider crabs, moray eels, sea turtles, and sea horses. The children will love to view the penguins from above and below as they crawl through clear underwater tunnels. These adorable water birds have an indoor and outdoor exhibit that can be seen from the Riverwalk.

The highlight of the aquarium is the Shark Lagoon, one of the longest shark tunnels in the world. Guests stand on a motorized walkway that carries them through a semi-circular tube in a U-shaped layout through a giant tank filled with nurse sharks and sawfish. The cool thing about it too is that not only do you get a great 180-degree underwater view but you can also go above the tank and appear straight down into it from a variety of angles enabling you to watch the shark fins pierce the water ala jaws. There is also a creepy and mysterious soundtrack playing in the background (all the background music is done really well here).

A sign outside Ripley's advertises it as "America's #1 Aquarium." I've never been there but I've always assumed the Georgia Aquarium to be the best, followed by the Monterey Bay Aquarium (which I have visited and is truly amazing). I wouldn't rate Ripley's the number one aquarium but it was slightly better than I expected it to be and is a good option if you're looking for an hour or two of entertainment and discovery. I'd also rate it a notch higher than its sister aquarium in Toronto. While the Shark Lagoon is an outstanding exhibit, the Aquarium of the Smokies as a whole lack that one unique, marquee animal that they can hang their hat on. For example, Monterey Bay has sea otters and the Georgia Aquarium has whale sharks, the Dig at Atlantis is home to manta rays, etc. Beyond the Shark Lagoon, there are really no imaginative tank designs (unlike Monterey Bay, which had several stunning designs). As an adult I did find enjoyment in visiting the Gatlinburg aquarium but it is really geared more towards kids. In the end, the aquarium is slightly overpriced (AAA members get a $1 off discount per ticket) but is a much better value than most of the other overpriced tourist traps in Gatlinburg and Pigeon Forge. The aquarium is a great backup plan if the weather turns sour. http://www.ripleyaquariums.com/gatlinburg/

Anakeesta ($$)

Gatlinburg is one of the most popular tourist destinations in the United States and it keeps getting bigger and better. One of the biggest and best additions has been Anakeesta. Opened in September 2017, Anakeesta is a self-described "outdoor family theme park" and is continuing to grow. Located on top of Anakeesta mountain on the east side of Gatlinburg, the most common way to get to the mountaintop park is by chondola – a chairlift/gondola hybrid. Visitors have the option of taking the open-air ski lift style chairs that can seat up to six or the enclosed red colored gondolas. There are only eight total enclosed cabins, so the wait can be quite lengthy for those. The ski lift is probably the longest period of time my kids have sat completely still without moving! The only other way to get to Anakeesta that I know of is the Ridge Rambler trucks.

The station for both options is located across the street from the Ripley's Aquarium. If you visit in the morning you could be staring into the sun for most of your trip up the mountain to Firefly Village, and the chairs could be wet from morning dew. The ride coming down is much better than going up as the views of Gatlinburg and surrounding area are fantastic.

The latest addition to Anakeesta is the AnaVista Tower. Opened in July 2020, visitors can climb the stairs and enjoy 360-degree views from downtown Gatlinburg's highest point. As of October 2020, the tower still is not 100% complete. There is an area where a glass floor will be installed so you can stare straight down at the ground sixty feet below.

Our kids loved Anakeesta. There's a whole area with climbing ropes and nets, all surrounded by wonderous views of the mountains. At Anakeesta, you can stroll along suspension bridge after suspension bridge. In fact, there are sixteen suspension bridges spanning a total of 800 feet through the trees.

The biggest negative to the day was actually right after leaving Anakeesta. We parked in the parking garage behind the aquarium across the street from the chairlift terminal. The traffic congestion was so bad it took more than a half an hour just to exit the garage and turn left onto US-441, a distance of ~0.25 miles. I guess that's what we get for visiting on a weekend in October.

Overall, we had a great time. If traffic/crowds weren't so bad we would've loved to go back later in the day as your lift pass is good all day long (instead we went hiking in the national park and saw a black bear just feet away from us). One of the additional upcharge attractions at Anakeesta is the Dueling Zipline Challenge that we did not do on our latest trip but sure looks fun. In its current form, Anakeesta is probably a half-day visit at best. A few more attractions or things to do at the top of the mountain to lengthen your experience and to get more value out of the lift ticket will really solidify Anakeesta as a must visit on every trip to the Smoky Mountains.

Rail Runner at Anakeesta($)

The first thing we did upon arriving at the top of Anakeesta's mountain was to grab a ticket to Rail Runner, the only single rail alpine coaster in North America. Unfortunately, after paying ~$22 for a lift ticket you have to pay an additional $12.99 to ride the coaster. Luckily, you can add a child passenger for only $2 more. If you are planning on riding Rail Runner, I recommend riding it early in the day as the low capacity of the coaster could lead to lengthy wait times later on.

This ride is one of the wildest and most intense alpine coasters I've been on. Unlike the other alpine rides in the area, this one has you board at the top and immediately plummet down the side of the mountain. It has a 400-foot elevation change over only a 1,600-foot downhill layout, which makes for some quick sudden drops and super-tight turns. It's short but it's intense if you go full throttle. The single rail definitely increases the sense of danger and thrill over its two rail companions. If it hadn't been for the seat belt, I was easily headed down the side of the mountain, this coaster is nuts!

Gatlinburg SkyBridge and SkyLift ($$)

Located at the top of the iconic SkyLift, the Gatlinburg SkyBridge is the longest pedestrian suspension bridge in North America and one of the most spectacular experiences in the Smokies. From the mountain-top SkyDeck, the SkyBridge quite literally crosses the sky as it stretches 680 feet across a deep valley in a single five-foot-wide span. Guests can walk across at their own pace, taking in the panoramic views and enjoying the spectacular setting before walking back when they're ready, or taking the newly constructed trail around. With a height of 150 feet at its midpoint, the SkyBridge is an incredible but easily attainable experience you'll never forger - especially as you cross the thirty feet of glass-floor panels in the middle of the span. The bridge is currently priced at $28 dollars for an adult. The Gatlinburg SkyBridge and Skylift park is definitely one to keep an eye on in the coming years. They are poised for growth and for adding even more attractions. I can't wait to see what the future holds!

https://www.gatlinburgskylift.com/skybridge

Roaring Fork Motor Trail (FREE)

One way to get a taste of the Great Smoky Mountains National Park without driving all the way to Cades Cove or Cherokee is to take the Roaring Fork Motor Trail in Gatlinburg. Named after Roaring Fork, one of the largest and fastest flowing mountain streams in the area, the motor trail is a six mile, paved, one way loop that will take you through old-growth forests and past historic buildings. Spotting animals is possible, though your chance of seeing wildlife may not be as high as in some other areas of the park due to its closer proximity to civilization. Roaring Fork features one of the most popular waterfalls in the Great Smoky Mountains National Park: Grotto Falls. The Trillium Gap Trail leads to the 25-foot-high Grotto Falls where you can walk behind a wall of water as it cascades to the ground. It's breathtakingly beautiful and the only spot in the Smokies where you can do this. The motor trail is closed during the winter months. Buses, trailers, and motor homes are not permitted on the motor nature trail. To access the trail, turn at traffic light #8 on the Parkway and follow the Historic Nature Trail-Airport Road into the national park.

http://www.nps.gov/grsm/planyourvisit/roaringfork.htm

Great Smoky Mountains National Park

The Great Smoky Mountains National Park is the most visited national park in the United States. In fact, in the year 2013 it had more than DOUBLE the number of visitors of the second most visited, Grand Canyon National Park, and had up to ten times more visitors than most of the other parks in the top ten. 12.5 million visitors made their way to the park in 2019. The park's location and accessibility are large factors; it's within a day's drive of a third of the population of the United States. Unlike some of the other popular national parks, GSMNP is free to enter.

Great Smoky Mountains National Park straddles the ridge line of the Great Smoky Mountains, which are a part of the Blue Ridge Mountain chain, a division of the even bigger Appalachian Mountain chain. The park was chartered by Congress in 1934 and officially dedicated by President FDR in 1940. It covers 522,419 acres and is one of the largest protected areas of the eastern United States. Main entrances are along U.S. Highway 441 at Gatlinburg, TN, and Cherokee, NC, or you can bypass all the tourist stuff entirely by entering the national park from Townsend or Cosby. The park gets its name because the trees emit a volatile organic compound during respiration that give off a blue haze that looks like smoke.

Today, the park activities enjoyed by visitors are quite varied and include hiking, backpacking, camping, fishing, horseback riding, bicycling, tubing, rock climbing and mountaineering. Visitors should be aware that permits are required for some park activities; you should check with park officials for all of the details and pricing for purchase of park permits. There's no hunting inside the park and to go fishing you need to apply for a fishing permit in a nearby town.

One of the highlights for many visitors is the opportunity to see wildlife. Large mammals residing in the park include black bear, deer, elk, wild hogs, coyotes, foxes, and river otters. Wild turkeys are commonly seen. The big attraction is, of course, the black bears. There are approximately 1,500 black bears living within GSMNP, or roughly two bears per square mile. When driving through the park, be on the lookout for "bear jams," traffic jams caused by bear sightings.

Remember to always fill up on gas before venturing into the park. Despite 270 miles of paved and gravel roads there are no public gas stations inside park boundaries. Drives may appear short on the maps, less than 30 miles, but be warned they are not quick; steep, winding two-lane roads with blind corners and narrow shoulders. Speed limits are generally 35 miles per hour or less. Some roads are closed during the winter months so be sure to stop by a visitor center to check which ones are open. Sometimes there are also occasional road closures due to construction, landslides, or other events.

http://www.nps.gov/grsm/index.htm

Tip: Set out early, before 10am when the roads get busier and the parking spots for trails fill up. 10am is usually when the first round of "pancake eaters" get done with their breakfasts and head out for a hike. Besides, it's advantageous to look for wildlife in the early morning and evening hours.

Visitor Centers

Spend an afternoon at one of the four visitor centers in the Great Smoky Mountains for special exhibits, to purchase park guides, or to meet with a park ranger. Each of the visitor centers has public restrooms within the buildings or nearby and bookshops for purchasing keepsakes. The Sugarlands Visitor Center is the most popular of the three in-park visitor centers. You'll find a museum about the plants and animals and a free-20-minute video about the history of the park. The Oconaluftee Visitor Center has a museum that replicates a farmhouse as well as other structures from days gone by, complete with demonstrations. Cades Cove Visitor Center has a grist meal that offers corn meal milling demonstrations and several log structures that can be explored.

Each of the visitor centers offers numerous ranger programs during spring, summer and fall, including a great Junior Rangers program, where kids ages five to twelve can earn a Junior Ranger's badge if they attend a certain number of programs.

Tip: There are no food vendors inside GSMNP. Pack your lunch to save extra time by avoiding having to leave the park to get something to eat.

Hiking

Hiking is a great way for families to escape and enjoy the outdoors together. The Great Smoky Mountains offer 800 miles of hiking trails, the only national parks with more are Yellowstone and Yosemite. While you can see much of what the park has to offer from your car, walking even short distances can put you in a totally different world.

Please be aware pets are prohibited on trails. In fact, when we were hiking that was how we knew there were bears close by: we saw their droppings littered all over the trails before we saw them.

Inside Great Smoky Mountain National Park, dogs are allowed in campgrounds, picnic areas, and along roads but they must remain on a leash at all times. There are only two trails where dogs are allowed to walk: the Gatlinburg Trail and the Oconaluftee River Trail. You must clean up after your pet and it is not advised to leave them unattended in vehicles or RVs.

Your cell phone will probably not get reception in most areas of the park, so do not rely on it for directions or to call for assistance. Always check the weather before you go out on the trails.

Tip: Decide how far you think you can hike before you set off. Allow enough time to complete the trip before nightfall. Generally, hikers in the Smokies average about 1.5 miles of trail per hour. If you are hiking with children your pace will probably be less so plan accordingly. It is advisable to carry drink water, raingear, and a flashlight while hiking the trails.

Waterfalls

The easiest waterfall in the park to access is Cataract Falls. To reach Cataract Falls from the Sugarlands Visitor Center, walk between the center and the restroom building. Follow the asphalt path to the Fighting Creek nature trail. Turn left onto the nature trails and follow it across Fighting Creek by taking the large wooden bridge. Turn right onto the trails to Cataract Falls and follow it until you reach the waterfall. The roundtrip distance to the falls and back to the visitor center is 0.8 miles. You probably won't see much wildlife here but it's an easy trail to start with and the babbling brook is quite relaxing to hear.

Once you reach Cataract Falls, keep going for a little bit. This part of the trail is the Cove Mountain Trail which eventually (after eight miles) links up with the Laurel Falls Trail. In October 2020, ten minutes on the Cove Mountain Trail past Cataract Falls and the busy tourist area, we stumbled upon a black bear! It's one thing to see a bear from the safety of your car but quite another to be feet away from one with nothing between you but dirt and leaves. Thankfully, this particular bear was more scared of us and scampered off into the woods upon hearing the sound of our surprised voices but it was a thrill to see one so close nonetheless.

Laurel Falls is one of the most popular destinations in the park. The trail gently ascends Cove Mountain and leads hikers to an eighty-foot, multi-level waterfall. The falls are named after mountain laurel, an evergreen shrub that grows in the region. The 1.3 miles from the parking area to the falls are paved due to the popularity of the hike. The trailhead and parking area is located just off of Little River Road approximately four miles from the Sugarlands Visitor Center, its accessibility another reason for its popularity. Go early in the morning or late in the day as the parking spaces fill up quickly. The more crowded an area is with people, the less likely you are going to see any wildlife.

Cades Cove

Cades Cove is the most popular region of the park and will see in excess of two million visitors every year. The highlight of Cades Cove is the 11-mile one way loop road that circles this isolated valley. If you're traveling from Pigeon Forge or Gatlinburg you should allow at least three hours to drive to Cades Cove, complete the loop, and drive back. Traffic moves very slowly, so plan on at least an hour to drive around the loop, but you'll want to take your time to savor the sights. Driving around inside the broad, green valley surrounded by mountains you'll find restored log cabins, barns, and churches. Halfway around the circle is the Cable Mill gristmill where you can find restrooms. Cades Cove may be your best opportunity to see wildlife: deer, bears, and wild turkeys are commonly seen. If you're lucky you might even spot a bobcat, fox, or coyote. Cades Cove is reserved for bicyclist and pedestrians only from sunrise until 10:00am every Wednesday and Saturday morning, May through September.

Tip: The main road into Cades Cove is the Little River Road, a long, winding road with a maximum speed limit of 45 miles per hour. The blind twists and headache inducing turns may seem endless, especially to younger travelers. A shortcut to bypass much of the spiraling road and cut the travel time down is to not enter the park from 441 but instead take Wears Valley Road (the same road the Alpine Coaster and Goats on the Roof are on) from Pigeon Forge until you reach Townsend. From Wears Valley Road (321) turn left onto E Lamer Alexander Pkwy (73) then turn right onto Laurel Creek Road.

Clingman's Dome

The most scenic vantage point in all of the Smokies is from the top of the observation tower at Clingman's Dome. From the parking area, it's a half mile hike up a paved but steep path before you reach the observation tower. Once you ascend the curved ramp to the top of the 45-foot-tall concrete observation tower you'll be at the highest point in the GSMNP at 6,643 feet. The incredible view is well worth the climb: limitless green forests stretch for miles; ridgelines plunge down into valleys and up to soft edged peaks shrouded in wispy white clouds. Visibility is as much as 100 miles on clear days. Air temperatures at Clingman's Dome generally are ten to twenty degrees cooler than the lower elevations like those at the visitor centers so bring an extra sweatshirt or jacket. The seven-mile-long road from Newfound Gap is open from April through November.

Tip: To encounter less crowds consider visiting during the "off-season." The peak tourist seasons are from June to August and the entire month of October.

Foothills Parkway (FREE)

Looking for a scenic drive that's not as long or as crowded as some of the more popular ones? Or one that'll take you somewhere that's not just a loop? I recommend driving the Foothills Parkway between US 321 in Walland to Wears Valley. This newest section of the parkway opened in December 2018 and is separate from the main national park area. The views are stunning, especially in the fall.

If you're leaving or entering the region from the North or West the parkway is another excellent alternative for avoiding the more crowded popular roads. Instead of driving east from Knoxville to Sevierville then south, drive south first to Maryville, then east on 321.

The Foothills Parkway extends even father to the southwest but I personally have not had the opportunity to check it out yet. One thing I love about the Smokies is there is always something to look forward to seeing on your next visit because it's nearly impossible to do it all in one trip.

Camping ($)

There are no hotels or cabin rentals located inside national park boundaries (other than LeConte Lodge which you have to hike to). If you want to stay overnight inside the park, you're going to have to rough it and go camping. There are ten campgrounds located inside the park with the largest being Elkmont, Cades Cove, and Cosby. At Big Creek, there are only twelve tent sites. Every campground has restrooms with running water and flush toilets but be warned there are no showers, electricity, or water hookups (the horror!). Campgrounds are smack dab in the middle of bear country thus all food must be stored out of sight in a closed vehicle. Camping in the Smokies is a star-gazer's dream and at only a fraction of the cost of a nearby hotel room or cabin.

Tip: To keep away from the crowds for a more intimate experience try visiting one of the less popular (and often harder to reach) areas of the park. Less visited areas are Abrams Creek, Balsam Mountain, Cosby, Fontana Lake, Greenbrier Cove, and Cataloochee.

Where to Stay ($-$$$)

There are literally thousands of hotel rooms in Pigeon Forge and Gatlinburg. Every price range and taste are available, from dirt cheap to several hundred dollars per night, from plain and generic to nicely themed experiences. A majority of the hotels in Pigeon Forge are located just off of the Parkway.

As far as location, personally I like to pick an area near the attractions I'm going to spend the most time at in order to cut down on driving time, even if that means paying a little more. If you're planning on spending a lot of time in Gatlinburg or the National Park, either stay in Gatlinburg proper or it might be a good idea to stay as far south on the Parkway as possible to save commuting time.

I've already mentioned the numerous camping options in and around the national park, but what about glamping? There are several places that offer camping-like experiences with a little more glamour, such as staying in a yurt or a luxury tent. If this interests you, check out Sky Ridge Yurts, Asheville Glamping, or Under Canvas Smoky Mountains.

A fun alternative to staying in a motel or hotel is to stay in a luxury cabin or chalet. Staying in a cabin could really take your vacation to the next level and make it a truly memorable experience. They're especially great for honeymoons or when traveling with friends or family. The mountain views are incredible, especially at sunset while soaking in the private hot tubs on the cabin's decks. Don't try to cram in too much each day. The whole point of renting a cabin is being able to lounge in your pajamas on the deck, watch a spectacular sunset, and cozy up by the fire. You may not want to leave the cabin at all - and that's perfectly fine.

The cost per night might be prohibitively expensive for some families on their own but a group of four or more can rent a nicer cabin with more amenities for a lower price per couple. Save money by brining your own food instead of eating out every night. If you're staying with friends it could be fun to have each couple plan and cook one nightly meal.

If you're thinking about staying in a cabin and are looking at prices, be aware of the potential "hidden" fees. If the cabin has a hot tub (and most do) there could be an additional hot tub fee that is not considered as part of the nightly rate. During the busy summer season, nearly every cabin will require your stay duration to be at least two nights and may charge a reservation fee. Then there are state and Sevier County taxes to potentially pay as well. So just be warned when you see that totally awesome Groupon deal that looks too good to be true, be sure to read all the fine print so you aren't caught by any unexpected fees.

Tip: Sometimes you can take advantage of the fact the cabins require guests to stay more than one night. For example, let's say you've booked Thursday through Saturday night, checking out Sunday morning and another couple booked the same cabin beginning Monday evening. This means Sunday night is unfilled but another guest can't book it because it's only available one night. The cabin company would rather have the cabin filled than sitting empty a night so you now have the opportunity to extend your stay by a night or two for a steep discount, at least 50% off, if not more!

Dollywood Cabins ($$$)

If you're planning on spending a day or more at Dollywood, I highly recommend staying in the Dollywood Cabins. They're a bit pricey and you need to book well in advance but it is totally worth it. Very good value and one of the best places I've ever stayed. Here are the top perks of staying in a Dollywood managed cabin:

Length of Stay Tickets: Guests staying in a cabin have the option of purchasing length of stay tickets, meaning you can visit the theme park every day for your entire stay. They also have length of stay passes that include TimeSaver, Dollywood's skip-the-line system. I love having the ability to visit the park for a few hours, leave and relax back at the cabin for the afternoon, then return to the park for Great Pumpkin Luminights or to see the Christmas lights.

Easy Access to Dollywood: Cabin guests receive FREE parking in a reserved lot at Dollywood separate from the main parking lot and FREE parking at Dollywood's Splash Country. Cabin guests get to use the private resort entrance into Dollywood which definitely helps speed up the entry process, especially with the additional temperature checks put into place due to the global pandemic. Cabin guests do NOT need reservations to get entry into Dollywood during the pandemic. Despite being only a few thousand feet from the train circle, by car it was a 6-mile drive from our cabin to the parking lot. But at least we could avoid driving down the very crowded main streets of Pigeon Forge.

The Views: Of course, not every cabin will have the same view, but ours was great. It was awesome being able to watch the sunrise over the Smoky Mountains. Some of the cabins look down upon Dollywood too.

Cabin Amenities: Our cabin was outfitted with several amenities such as an outdoor hot tub, pool table, air hockey, two fireplaces, and more. Another benefit is guests of the cabins can experience a select ride or attraction early each Saturday morning at the Dollywood Theme Park. For our latest visit it was the wing coaster, Wild Eagle.

Bring the whole family: There are cabins of all different shapes and sizes, ranging from one to seven bedrooms. The initial cost may be a shock but if you're splitting it among a group of friends or family it's really not any more expensive than the average hotel.

Location: I love the location of the cabins relative to everything else in the area. You're at the southern end of the Pigeon Forge so you can be in Gatlinburg or Smoky Mountain National Park very quickly and easily while avoiding a lot of the traffic lights and traffic jams. You'll have easy access to all the alpine coasters in the Smokies.

Returning Guest Discount: Once you stay in a cabin, you'll definitely want to come back. I don't think it's well advertised but returning guests get a 15% discount!

Dollywood's DreamMore Resort ($$$)

A big component of Dollywood's ten year, 300 million dollar investment plan announced in August 2013 was the creation of their first resort hotel, DreamMore, which began accepting reservations during summer 2015. On one of our visits to the area, we stayed at one of Dollywood's amazing Smoky Mountain Cabins and were really blown away. For DreamMore, we were expecting the same level of quality experienced at Dollywood and the cabins and we were not disappointed. When I first heard the name of the resort, I thought it was a bit odd. But it's grown on me, especially after I saw that the phrase "Dream More" is one of four pillars the hotel theme is built on: Do More. Learn More. Care More. Dream More.

Maybe the best way I can describe the appearance of the outside of the hotel is it's like a combination of Walt Disney World's Wilderness Lodge combined with The Grand Floridian. The entrance walkway itself is very reminiscent of Royal Pacific at Universal Orlando with a waterfall to your left as you walk over the rushing water. The grounds have many rock and water features scattered about. On a clear day you can see the Smoky Mountains in the distance. The hotel sits atop a large hillside so the lobby and gift shop are actually on the second floor. The restaurant, spa, pool, and game room are all on the first floor.

The rooms themselves are very well designed. The decorations and colors really work together to create a fun but laid back and relaxing atmosphere. I really appreciated how many places there were to hang or store your items.

While the outdoor pool area looks amazing, the indoor pool leaves a lot to be desired. It's essentially the same plain, boring pool you would find at any other hotel in the area. At a resort where everything else is done so well and to the next level, it's a bit disappointing the indoor pool doesn't have a little something to make it more special.

I also found it odd that there are no public microwaves in the entire resort. That's right, the rooms don't have them and when we asked a staff member, we were told there are none we could use. What if you have baby formula or something that has to be warmed up?

While staying at DreamMore may be a bit more expensive than the Comfort Inn down the street, the additional perks make it worth it if you're planning on visiting Dollywood or Splash Country. There is a complimentary trolley service to both parks and they usually have two to three trolleys operating whenever Dollywood is open, starting a half hour before and ending a half hour after the park closes. You'll also get early Saturday entry, one hour before the park opens to the public, use of special "side" entrance into Dollywood, a TimeSaver pass to skip the lines, and two-day admission for the price of one. Check the resort's website prior to booking to double-check the latest perks.

What are the advantages of staying at DreamMore versus a Dollywood cabin? While the cabins may have a better view and feel more isolated, DreamMore has that amazing outdoor pool and the free transportation to the theme park. The hotel is a lot easier to find than the cabins too, and you can reach the other attractions in the area a lot quicker from the hotel.

Overall, I was very impressed with Dollywood's DreamMore Resort. It's a beautiful hotel in a great setting and the people that work there are some of the nicest you'll ever meet. I highly recommend checking it out, especially if you're going to be spending any time at Dollywood as the extra perks are well worth it.

In March of 2020, Dollywood was scheduled to make a huge announcement about the largest investment plan in their history. Most likely about the addition of a second resort. However, the announcement was cancelled the day before the press event due to the global pandemic and their plans seemed to have been delayed by at least one year. It may take longer, but I expect Dollywood to add another hotel and maybe even extend their operating season even longer than it already is.

Margaritaville Island Hotel ($$$)

One of the more unique hotels I've ever seen is inspired by the lyrics and lifestyle of singer, songwriter, and author, Jimmy Buffet: the Margaritaville Island Hotel. Located inside The Island at Pigeon Forge, the guest rooms reside mostly on the second floor above The Island's shops and restaurants. The hotel's pool is even situated on the roof of a building, and can be seen from the Smoky Mountain Skywheel. Staying at the hotel comes with several unique perks, from upgraded amenities such as fireplaces and private balconies along the Little Pigeon River, to the "Frozen Concoction Maker" available in every room for creating your own signature drinks. The Island is a great location to base your Smoky Mountain vacation out of. It's toward the Southern end of the Pigeon Forge "strip" with Gatlinburg and the national park just down the road.

When to Visit

Each season in the Great Smoky Mountain Region brings unique opportunities and activities. In the spring the mountains explode with green color and the bears come out of hibernation. Dolly Parton usually has her homecoming parade in early May. Summer brings car shows and Fourth of July celebrations but is also the rainy season.

One event that I've not yet made it to that's at the top of my bucket list is the annual viewing of the synchronous fireflies. Synchronous fireflies (Photinus carolinus) are one of at least 19 species of fireflies that live in Great Smoky Mountains National Park. They are the only species in America whose individuals can synchronize their flashing light patterns! The mating season lasts for approximately two weeks each year. The dates that the fireflies begin to display varies from year to year but is typically around the third week of May to the third week in June. Because of the high demand and limited space, there is a lottery, usually around April, to get tickets to see the amazing nature display. https://www.nps.gov/grsm/learn/nature/fireflies.htm

One of the most popular times to visit is in October, the middle of fall season. The color changes of the forest leaves are quite remarkable and really pull in the crowds. Peak tree color occurs earlier in the higher elevations and becomes later as you get lower. It's also rutting season for the elk and you might be able to hear the bugling of the bulls.

Early winter is quickly becoming a favorite time to visit the Smokies based on two events that keep getting bigger and better year after year. The first is Pigeon Forge's Winterfest, a four-month long celebration featuring more than five million Christmas lights scattered throughout the area. Winterfest usually occurs mid-November through February. Pick up your driving tour guide brochure at the Pigeon Forge Welcome Center at traffic light #0 or at the Fun Time Trolley office in Patriot Park.

Smoky Mountain Christmas at Dollywood has won the Golden Ticket Award for Best Christmas Event more than eight years in a row. The theme park is decked with Christmas decorations – even in areas where you wouldn't expect them. Your family will love all the numerous, fun photo opportunity areas. You can get your picture taken inside a snow globe, inside a giant wreath in front of the train, under a mistletoe, with Santa Claus or a character from Rudolph the Red-nosed Reindeer. And the buildings covered in over four million lights are such a beautiful sight to behold. Almost all of the rides will still be running too – minus the water rides of course.

Great Smoky Mountain National Park Attendance

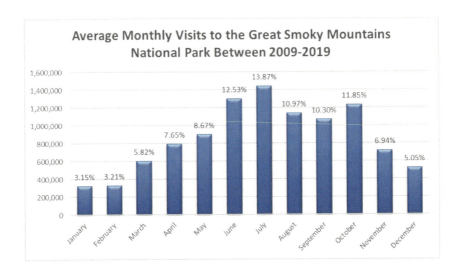

The top five busiest months for the Great Smoky Mountains National Park (according to data compiled between 2009 and 2019) are:

1. July
2. June
3. October
4. August
5. September

The least five busiest months are:

1. January
2. February
3. December
4. March
5. November

https://www.nps.gov/grsm/learn/management/ves.htm#:~:text=Great%20Sm oky%20Mountains%20National%20Park%20is%20situated%20within%20a%20day's,12.5 %20million%20times%20in%202019.

Gatlinburg Yearly Weather

To give you a quick idea on the weather, I've put together some climate data for the town of Gatlinburg.

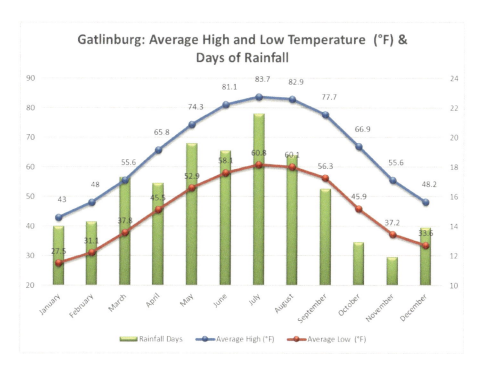

The warmest months of the year are:

1. July
2. August
3. June
4. September
5. May

The coldest months of the year are:

1. January
2. February
3. December
4. November
5. March

The five wettest months of the year are:

1. July
2. May
3. June
4. August
5. March

The three driest months in terms of rainfall are:

1. November
2. October
3. December

https://www.weather-us.com/en/tennessee-usa/gatlinburg-climate#rainfall_days

Things to do before you Travel

Proper planning is important for any vacation and you can prevent headaches, problematic situations, and save time by running through this list of important to-dos before you leave.

Check your shoes

Brand new shoes often aren't the best idea to take on vacation. If you're going to buy new shoes do so several weeks before your travel date so they're nice and broken in by the time you depart for vacation. You don't want sore or feet while on vacation. An easy alternative to buying and breaking in new shoes is to simply get new inserts to add some padding to kicks you already know and love.

Camera check

Double check your camera and cell phone to ensure your batteries are charged. Make room for all the great photographs you're going to take. Whether you're using a digital camera or a smart phone for your vacation pictures, make sure your memory card is good and empty before you arrive. You may even want to invest in a spare memory card or batteries.

Check your sunscreen

Double check all your sunscreen before you depart. If you can't find an expiration date on the sunscreen bottle, play it safe and buy a new bottle. If you're not used to standing outside all day, the sun can be particularly brutal. Reapply sunscreen often, several times a day. If you're hesitant to slather on a greasy lotion that could mess up your makeup, look for sunscreen that's formulated just for the face.

Tentatively plan your days

It's a good idea to have a general plan of what you're doing each day of your trip. Take some time and really explore your options so you don't waste any time unnecessarily. Now, don't plan your trip down to every last minute because things will never go exactly according to plan. You need to have room to maneuver around all the little hiccups that are sure to occur due to the thousands of variables: weather, unexpected attraction closures, etc. While you're bound to run into unexpected delays or surprisingly shorter travel times, it's a good idea to have at least a general idea of what you want see, do, eat, and buy so you can make the most of your time and money on vacation. Make lists in order of priority of all the places you want to visit – which ones will you be heartbroken if you don't get to do and which ones would you be OK if you have to end up skipping them.

Prepare a first aid kit

While first aid is readily available at most attractions, it's still nice to have a few necessities on hand yourself. Consider the unique conditions you'll face out on the trails and plan accordingly. If you're a thrill seeker, roller coasters and loud shows can easily give you a headache. Bumpy rides, greasy foods, and hot weather can leave you feeling nauseous. Head off predictable problems with preventative medications for motion sickness or heartburn if you know you're prone to these conditions. Band-Aids are a must, especially if traveling with children.

Aloe and vitamin E will do wonders for tender skin after a long day in the sun. Heating or cooling pads can help with sore muscles and bandages can save painful feet if you didn't heed the warning about shoes and wore a troublesome pair anyway.

Wear a mask and other global pandemic tips

Beginning in 2020 during the COVID-19 global pandemic, most if not all the attractions in the area require visitors to wear facial coverings in compliance with national and local safety guidelines. Even as vaccines begin to be rolled out at the start of 2021, mask wearing will more than likely continued to be required for some time. Be sure to bring extra masks as you may want to swap out multiple times a day during hot weather.

With the COVID 19 global pandemic, it's especially important to check the websites of any attractions you want to visit to read about their latest safety procedures. Some may require you to make reservations in advance, so you'll want to double check to make sure you don't miss out on any fun. Read park policies before visiting. Every park's website should have its policies easily accessible from the homepage. As mentioned above, these will vary from park to park. However, common measures include:

Advanced reservations to enter the park
Temperature checks and health screenings upon arrival
Virtual queues
Face masks mandatory (check to see if they have criteria for specific types of masks or what age ranges are required to wear them)
No paper maps (download park apps before visiting)
Reduced or modified operating dates and hours

Subscribe to Websites, Social Media, and Reward Programs

For the latest news, potential savings, special events, promotions, etc. subscribe to an attraction's newsletter or social media accounts. Download their mobile app if they have one and become familiar with it. This way you'll know well ahead of time if something comes up and you can adjust your schedule accordingly. In addition, you should sign up for any reward programs that are available to you. For instance, if you're staying in a Choice Hotel (Comfort Inn, Quality Suites, Clarion, etc.) you can earn reward points towards a free night on your next vacation very easily.

While it's great to leave room for spontaneity and new discoveries, these important tasks will help you stay comfortable on your trip and make the most of every minute.

Enjoy Your Vacation

Winter can be a long and brutal season for those of us living in the northern United States. We endure a cold and snowy winter that limits our outdoor activities. November to March is a long, long time and undoubtedly come January or February, the dreaded "Winter Withdrawal Syndrome" sets in. Many of us "snow birds" head south for a bit of a respite during the holidays. This helps but is only a temporary reprieve. It's not long before we get cabin fever. All too soon we're back up to our knees in snow and longing for the outdoors and warmer weather. The first chance we get we head south. Every year, around March or April, with Spring right around the corner many of us get that travel "itch." A great way to fulfil that itch is by traveling to the Smoky Mountains.

I hope you've enjoyed reading ***Things to do in the Smokies with Kids***. I firmly believe that the investment of even the shortest family excursion, even a day trip, will reward you and your family with experiences and memories that will last a lifetime. One of the best pieces of advice I've ever received for living a happy life is "always have something to look forward to." Imagine you and your family planning a trip to the Smoky Mountains, talking it over, and getting everyone excited. Planning your trip is part of the fun as you anticipate all your future adventures. I hope my tips have been helpful. You've got a fun journey ahead of you.

Did You Like Things to Do in the Smokies with Kids?

Before you go, I'd like to say "thank you" for purchasing my book. I know you could have picked from dozens of other books but you took a chance on mine. So, a big thanks for ordering this book and reading all the way to the end! You're awesome.

Now I'd like to ask for a *small* favor. Could you please take a minute or two and leave a review for this book on Amazon.com? Your comments are really valuable because they will guide future editions of this book and I'm always striving to improve my writing. I will constantly be updating and releasing new editions of this guide as I discover more fun things to do. Please let me know if there is an attraction I missed out on.

The 50 Most Terrifying Roller Coasters Ever Built

Mega roller coasters of today reach heights of over 400 feet and speeds in excess of 100 miles per hour. Roller coasters towering taller than a certain height are terrifying for many individuals but it would be boring to simply make a list of the world's tallest coasters. As a result, most of the bone-chilling machines in this thrilling book do not use sheer height to terrify, but instead prey on our fears and emotions in other, more creative ways. One element alone may not make a ride terrifying but the sum of all of its parts does. What factors make a roller coaster terrifying? Height, speed, inversions, backwards segments, unique track elements, darkness, and unexpected surprises all contribute to making your head spin and your knees tremble.

Where are the most terrifying roller coasters found? Who designs them? Which park builds the craziest rides? Find out by reading **The 50 Most Terrifying Roller Coasters Ever Built** by Nick Weisenberger, author of **Things to Do in the Smokies with Kids.**

"This is a fantastic book that gives great insight and ideas of where to travel for harrowing and fun-filled roller coaster experiences - it gave me an adrenaline rush just reading about the possibilities. " –Dexter, Amazon Reviewer, December 2014

"My roller coaster loving son thoroughly enjoyed this book. Easily broken down by ride with fun and pertinent facts about each coaster." – Lisa, Amazon Reviewer, August 2015

About the Author

Nick Weisenberger is an avid and experienced traveler. He loves to visit theme parks, zoos, and national parks – just another reason why he can't stop visiting the Great Smoky Mountain region. When not writing or working, Nick likes to make Excel spreadsheets, read, hike, watch football, and explore. Look for him out on the trails or midways.

(me and my son in 2014)

Works by Nick Weisenberger

Coasters 101: An Engineer's Guide to Roller Coaster Design

25 Extreme Drop Tower Rides

Coaster Phobia

The 50 Most *Terrifying* Roller Coasters Ever Built

The 50 Most *Unique* Roller Coasters Ever Built

50 *Groundbreaking* Roller Coasters:
The Most Important Scream Machines Ever Built

50 *Legendary* Roller Coasters That No Longer Exist

The 50 Biggest Ferris Wheels Ever Built

Things to Do in the Smokies with Kids

76 Excel Tips to Increase Your Productivity and Efficiency

Once I was Adopted

Appendix I: Vacation Packing Checklist

Below is a handy list of items to remember to bring with you on a trip to the Smoky Mountain region:

GPS
GPS Charger
Cell phone
Cell Phone Charger
Camera
Camera Charger
Spare Batteries
Spare Memory Cards
Contact lenses
Deodorant
First aid kit
Hairdryer
Insect repellent
Prescription medications
Razors
Shampoo
Sunscreen
Toothbrush
Toothpaste

Binoculars
Brochures
Cash
Lodging and attraction addresses
Magazine/book/Kindle
Maps
Reservation numbers
Small stroller (easy to navigate through the crowded streets of Gatlinburg)
Snacks
Tickets
Water bottle
Hat
Hiking shoes
Jacket
Sunglasses
Swimsuit

Appendix II: Tools and Resources

List of resources and attractions found mentioned in this guide:

Pigeon Forge & Sevierville Attractions
Comedy Barn Show: https://comedybarn.com/
Country Tonite Show: https://www.countrytonitepf.com
Crave Golf: https://www.cravegolf.com/
Dollywood: http://www.dollywood.com/themepark
Fun Time Trolley: http://www.pigeonforgetrolley.org/
Goats on the Roof: http://www.goatsontheroofofthesmokies.com/
Hatfield and McCoy show: https://hatfieldmccoydinnerfeud.com/
Lost Treasure Golf: http://losttreasuregolf.com/miniature-golf-courses/pigeon-forge-mini-golf-course/
Old Mill: http://www.old-mill.com/
Paula Deen's Lumberjack Feud: https://lumberjackfeud.com/
Pirates Voyage Dinner Show: https://piratesvoyage.com/pigeon-forge/
Ripley's Golf: https://www.ripleys.com/gatlinburg/mini-golf/
Rocky Top Mountain Coaster: https://www.rockytopcoaster.com/
Rowdy Bear Ridge – Pigeon Forge:
https://www.rowdybearmountain.com/pigeon-forge/
Smoky Mountain Alpine Coaster:
http://www.smokymountainalpinecoaster.com/
Splash Country: http://www.dollywood.com/waterpark
The Island: http://islandinpigeonforge.com/

Gatlinburg Attractions
Gatlinburg Attractions: http://www.attractions-gatlinburg.com/
Gatlinburg Mountain Coaster:
http://gatlinburgmountaincoaster.com/
Gatlinburg SkyLift and SkyBridge:
https://www.gatlinburgskylift.com/skybridge
Ober Gatlinburg: http://www.obergatlinburg.com/
Ripley's Aquarium of the Smokies:
http://www.ripleyaquariums.com/gatlinburg/

Roaring Fork Motor Trail:
http://www.nps.gov/grsm/planyourvisit/roaringfork.htm
Rowdy Bear Mountain – Gatlinburg:
https://www.rowdybearmountain.com/gatlinburg/

Others
Cherokee: http://www.cherokee-nc.com/
Great Smoky Mountains National Park:
http://www.nps.gov/grsm/index.htm
https://www.nps.gov/grsm/learn/nature/fireflies.htm

Other Helpful Websites
Choice Hotels: http://www.choicehotels.com/
Coaster101: http://www.coaster101.com
Gatlinburg weather: https://www.weather-us.com/en/tennessee-usa/gatlinburg-climate#rainfall_days
Groupon: http://www.groupon.com/
Observation Wheel Directory:
http://www.observationwheeldirectory.com
Pigeon Forge Car Show schedule: http://pigeonforgerodruns.com/
Roller Coaster Database: http://www.rcdb.com
TripAdvisor: http://www.tripadvisor.com/

Made in the USA
Monee, IL
11 March 2022